NAUGHTY NORSKA

Written by Yvonne Horsfield
Illustrations by Garth Horsfield

Bumblebee Books
London

Belongs to

There is no doubt about it! This young pup was just a naughty street kid! She had no collar and no name. If she did have a home, it seemed that she did not want to be there. She wanted company and not an empty yard. Every day, she would wander the streets, sniffing out the scraps she could find and always ending up at the school yard. She had a beautiful Malamute face, but it looked too large for her thin, bony body. She knew that the children just loved her visits and they would share their lunches with her when she was so hungry.

Alas, the school principal was not happy! Every time she came he would ring the council pound and say, "Please come and take this pup away. She is a nuisance in the playground."

Three times the Pound man had taken her away and this time he said, "This will be the last time. She will probably be 'put down'!"

Now this was no ordinary pup; she was clever. She sat quietly by the van door and looked up at the circle of children, with her beautiful face and golden eyes, simply begging someone to save her.

Just as she was being lifted into the van, a young boy raced up, crying urgently, "Stop please! Someone wants to see her." He had run to ask the new teacher, Miss Evie, for help. "Please Miss, do come and save her — you haven't got a dog and I know you like her. Please, please Miss!"

COUNCIL
POUND

Reluctantly, Miss Evie approached the van, wishing she had not agreed to come. There she was, a sad and woebegone sight, with her bones sticking out all over. She was not the sort of dog that Miss Evie had in mind, but she could not turn away from those beautiful, golden eyes which begged her for mercy, as if she knew that she was on 'death row'.

Miss Evie considered that it was the last kind of dog she needed. "Too big! It will be nothing but trouble," she said to herself.

But despite the voice in her head which said, "NO!" VERY LOUDLY, there was a more insistent small voice in her heart which said, "YES!"

"Oh a-a-alright, I will take her home with me," she could hardly believe her own voice!

"Thank you, thank you Miss," the young boy cried, his face lit up with relief. "She will be a good dog," he said. "I wish I was allowed to have her."

Miss Evie at that moment was not quite so sure. Already, she regretted her hasty words. "I suppose you will need a name," she thought as she drove homewards from school with the pup cowering under the front seat. "As you're a Malamute or snow dog breed, I think Norska suits you quite well – yes, Norska it is!"

The Vet examined her next day and said, "You will have your hands full with this one. Although she is only about five or six months old, she will have learnt some bad habits and she has a mind of her own. You must be very strict with her, because this breed is extremely strong willed and stubborn."

In the year that followed, Miss Evie was to remember those words often. At every opportunity, Norska would be up to something! She still wanted to be free, and do what she pleased, just like the 'street kid' she used to be. Like 'Houdini' she would climb or dig to escape from the yard and many times, she would once again end up at the dog pound. Only this time, there was an owner ready to pay the fine.

"Why do I keep rescuing you?" Miss Evie asked herself in despair. "You are keeping me poor." But it was that special look from those golden eyes in Norska's beautiful face that gave her hope. "I know there's a good dog in you somewhere," she said. Norska agreed and gave a throaty yodel back to her.

One day Miss Evie almost gave up on her. This was definitely Norska's last chance! Miss Evie needed to do some shopping and decided it would be alright for Norska to come for the ride.

"Hop in the back girl," she said. It would only be a few minutes in the supermarket, as there was not much to get. She quickly bought what she needed and made her way back to the car. "Oh No!" she gasped in shock and dismay at the sight of her car. In protest at being left alone and unable to escape, Norska had ripped up the vinyl covering on the back seat to shreds! "You bad girl!" Miss Evie shouted, not quite knowing whether to laugh or cry. "What am I going to do with you?"

That night, Miss Evie felt very troubled, because although Norska had caused her so much mischief, she had grown to love her company, especially at night. She always felt safe with her curled up beside the bed.

"This is your very last chance to show me that you can be good," she said, with tears in her eyes. She didn't want to take Norska back to the pound. Norska put her head on Miss Evie's lap and looked up at her sorrowfully, with her beautiful golden eyes. She seemed to know that she may lose the best friend she would ever have, unless she could behave better.

That night, Miss Evie stoked up the fire and went to bed early. "Goodnight Norska," she said, patting her head and stroking her velvet ears. "I have a busy day at school tomorrow." Norska raised her head and yodeled back her own doggy response, then curled up on her special mattress beside the bed. Soon they were both fast asleep.

Hours later, Norska woke up suddenly and sniffed the air. Quietly, she crept into the passage and realized that something was wrong, the smell was getting much stronger. Ahead of her, black smoke was pouring out of the doorway from the living room! Quickly Norska turned back, barking loudly and racing to the bedroom where Miss Evie was still asleep in bed. She jumped onto the bed and Miss Evie woke with a start. "Quiet Norska! What is the matter with you? You are never so noisy and naughty like this at night time. Get off the bed!" she scolded.

Norska pulled at the bedclothes and licked her face until Miss Evie climbed crossly out of bed saying, "What's wrong with you?" Norska ran to the open door and as Miss Evie followed, she gained a whiff of the smoke now traveling down the passageway towards the bedroom. "Oh, my goodness, the house is on fire," she screamed in fright. Just as the flames were bursting through the doorway and into the passage, she realized that they must escape quickly.

With Norska close behind her and with shaking hands, she unlocked the front door and raced outside. Already the roof was burning and she could hear the siren of a fire truck wailing towards her in the distance.

In just minutes the fire truck had arrived and there were firemen quickly pumping water from the large hoses onto the burning building. Because it was an old wooden house, it was now burning fiercely and Miss Evie trembled with fright at the thought of what may have happened to her if Norska had not woken her so soon.

Gradually, many neighbours gathered around to see what was happening. Both she and Norska were taken into the house across the road and she was wrapped in a blanket and given a warm cup of strong tea, with Norska still close by her side. "You are my hero Norska!" she said, hugging her around the neck and stroking those velvet ears.

"Yes, you are so lucky to have such a faithful, clever dog" said her neighbour. "A few minutes more and you may have been trapped inside. She has saved you both."

From that moment, Miss Evie realized that she could never part with Norska, no matter how naughty she could sometimes be. But the strangest thing of all is that never again did Norska run away, dig holes, climb fences or destroy another thing! She had finally decided her home was with Miss Evie, and from that day she never left. Miss Evie had become her special friend and family forever.

About the Author & Illustrator

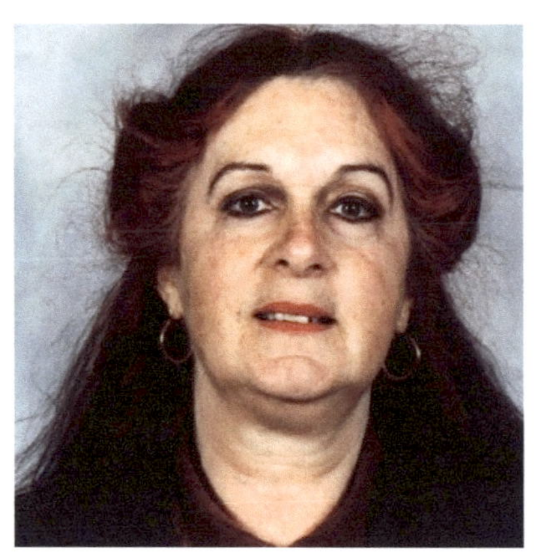

Yvonne has a background in teaching children in out-of-school situations such as Sovereign Hill Goldmining Township and the Art Gallery of Ballarat, plus added experience in schools teaching Italian language. She lives on a 3 acre bush block opposite State forest on the fringe of Ballarat and is passionate about wildlife and the natural environment. She has previously published several books on this theme and also loves all domestic animals. She has participated in many Book Week programs in local and Victorian schools.

Garth also inherited a love of animals and Nature's creations. From an early age he loved to sketch from reality as well as create from his imagination. His favorite Australian artist was Michael Leunig, cartoonist and satirist, famous for the wry humour evident in his sketches. Garth has practiced as a professional graphic artist for many years and also writes and performs his own music.

Dedication

In Loving Memory of Norska.